Overview *Stars of the Show*

Maya's second-grade class puts on a school play.

Reading Vocabulary Words

set
script
actors

High-Frequency Words

learn	*turn*
work	*show*
play	*goes*
begin	*party*

Building Future Vocabulary

* *These vocabulary words do not appear in this text. They are provided to develop related oral vocabulary that first appears in future texts.*

Words:	*titles*	*scenery*	*cast*
Levels:	Gold	Purple	Library

Comprehension Strategy
Rereading text

Fluency Skill
Reading smoothly

Phonics Skill
Changing phonemes to create word families *-ig* (big — dig), *-ight* (light — night), *-ake* (take — cake)

Reading-Writing Connection
Writing a journal entry

Home Connection
Send home one of the Flying Colors Take-Home books for children to share with their families.

Differentiated Instruction
Before reading the text, query children to discover their level of understanding of the comprehension strategy — Rereading text. As you work together, provide additional support to children who show a beginning mastery of the strategy.

Focus on ELL

- Draw a star and ask children to identify it. Discuss alternate meanings for the word *star* as a light in the sky or an actor.

- Explain that many words have more than one meaning. Discuss multiple meanings of the words *show* and *set*.

T1

Using This Teaching Version

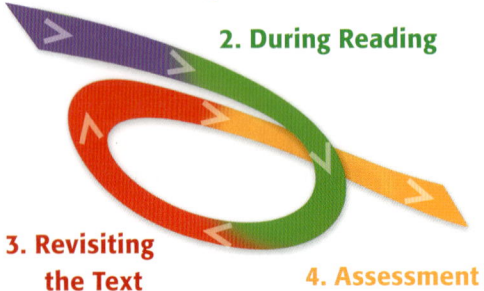

1. Before Reading
2. During Reading
3. Revisiting the Text
4. Assessment

This Teaching Version will assist you in directing children through the process of reading.

1. **Begin with Before Reading** to familiarize children with the book's content. Select the skills and strategies that meet the needs of your children.

2. **Next, go to During Reading** to help children become familiar with the text, and then to read individually on their own.

3. **Then, go back to Revisiting the Text** and select those specific activities that meet children's needs.

4. **Finally, finish with Assessment** to confirm children are ready to move forward to the next text.

1 Before Reading

Building Background
- Write the word *actors* on the board. Read it aloud. Have children share what they know about actors. Correct any misinformation.
- Introduce the book by reading the title, talking about the cover illustration, and sharing the overview.

Building Future Vocabulary
Use Interactive Modeling Card: Meaning Map
- Write the word *cast* on the Meaning Map Interactive Modeling Card. Add the sentence *The cast must learn lines.* Ask children what *cast* means. Write their definition on the card.
- Tell children they will learn another meaning for the word *cast* as they read *Stars of the Show.*

Introduction to Reading Vocabulary
- On blank cards write: *set*, *script*, and *actors*. Read them aloud. Tell children these words will appear in the text of *Stars of the Show.*
- Use each word in a sentence for understanding.

Introduction to Comprehension Strategy

Use Activity Sheet: Questions and Answers Chart

- Explain that sometimes going back to reread helps readers follow the events in a story.
- Tell children they will reread text to better understand what happens in *Stars of the Show*.
- Tell children they will be filling in a Questions and Answers Chart after reading the story. Have them think of questions as they read.

Introduction to Phonics

- Write **cart** on the board and use it in a sentence. Ask *What word will we get if we change the /k/ to /p/ at the beginning of this word?* (**part**) *What letter stands for /p/?* Erase the c in **cart** and write p at the beginning of **art**.

Modeling Fluency

- Read aloud page 2. Say *That was reading smoothly.* Reread page 2, pausing to take a breath mid-sentence. Ask *Was that reading smoothly? Why?* (No, you took a breath at the wrong time.)
- Point out that good readers look ahead as they read so they can read smoothly and know when to pause and take a breath.

2 During Reading

Book Talk

Beginning on page T4, use the During Reading notes on the left-hand side to engage children in a book talk. On page 24, follow with Individual Reading.

T3

During Reading

Book Talk

- Discuss the cover illustration. Encourage children to make predictions about what the play is about. (a dog)

- Ask *Is that a real dog in the picture?* (no) Discuss how one of the actors is playing the part of a dog.

Turn to page 2 – Book Talk

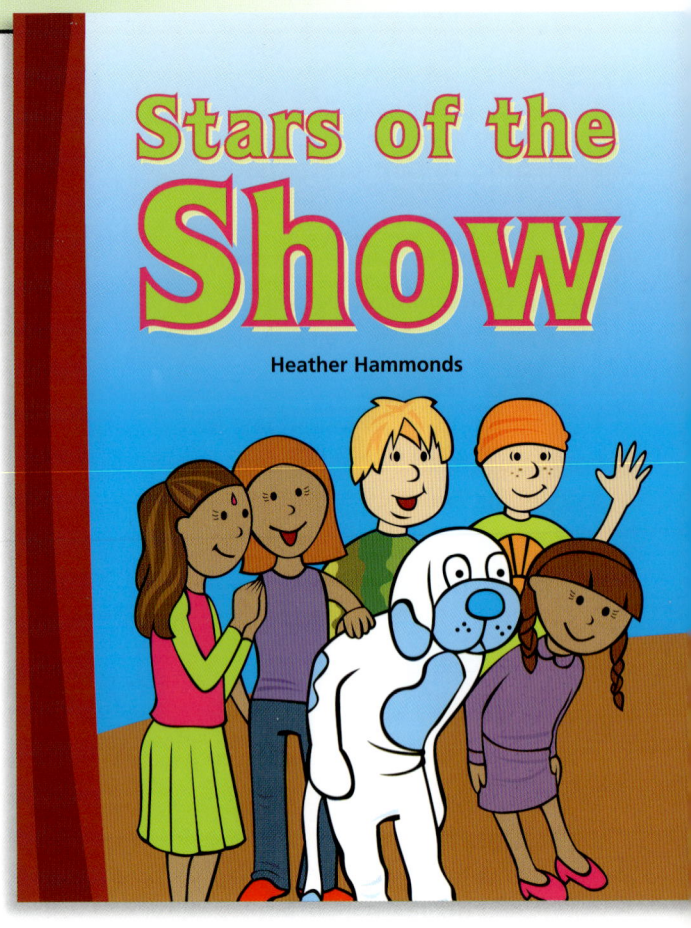

Revisiting the Text

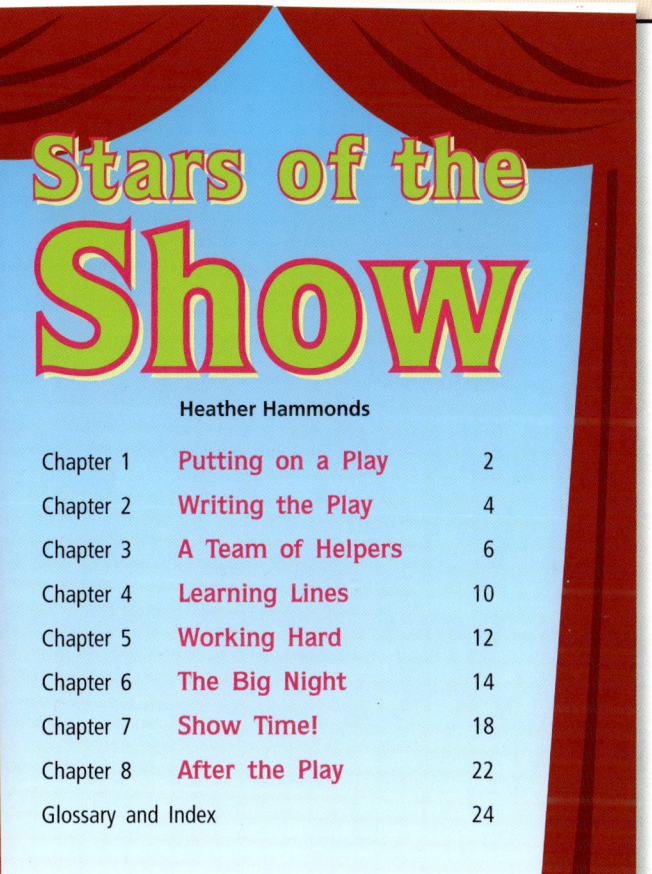

Future Vocabulary
- Point to page 1 and ask *Who knows what this page is called?* (contents page) Discuss this text feature with children. Show children examples from other books, if available, so they can see how contents pages are similar (chapter titles, page numbers) and how they are different (layout, content).

- Say *There are titles for each chapter. What color are the titles?* (pink) *What other things have titles?* (movies, books, people)

Now revisit pages 2–3

During Reading

Book Talk

- Have children point to the actors in the photograph on page 2. Then have them locate the word *actors* on the page. Remind children that words in dark letters, or boldfaced type, are in the glossary. Have children look up *actors* in the glossary and then use the word in a sentence.

- Ask children to describe a time they watched a play. Encourage them to include details about the experience. Ask *Has anyone ever been in a play?* Have children give details about how they helped to put on a play.

- Have children read page 3. Then say *I wonder what kind of play they will put on.* Suggest that children write this question on their Questions and Answers Chart.

Turn to page 4 – Book Talk

Putting on a Play

Have you ever been to a play?
A play is a kind of story.

The story is told by **actors** on a **stage**.

Revisiting the Text

Maya's class is putting on a play. Their teacher is helping them.

Future Vocabulary

- Discuss alternate meanings for the word *titles*. Say *People can have titles, too.*

- Discuss when you use the titles *Mr., Mrs., Ms.,* and *Dr.* Discuss how using titles is a way to show respect. For example, children may use titles when speaking to their teacher or the principal.

- Explain that titles can describe people's jobs at a company. Give examples of job titles, such as Senior Accountant or Administrative Assistant.

Now revisit pages 4–5

During Reading

Book Talk

- Introduce the word *script*. Say the word and point to it on page 4. Say *Actors speak the words that are written in the script for the play.* Direct children's attention to page 5. Say *This is a picture of a page from a script.* Explain that the names in a script refer to the names of the characters and not the actors' real names. Ask *Why don't authors write the actors' names in the script?* (They don't know who is going to be in the play when they write it.)

- Point to the sentences written in italics, or slanted letters, and explain that these are directions about what the actors are doing. Point to the other text and explain that these are the words the actors say. Discuss how text features such as boldfaced and italic type can help you understand a script or other text.

Turn to page 6 — Book Talk

Chapter 2
Writing the Play

Maya's class is writing their own play. Everyone makes up part of the story.

The teacher writes the play on some paper. This is called a play **script**.

4

Revisiting the Text

There are people and animals in the play. The play is about a dog who wants to fly!

The Dog Who Wanted to Fly

Digger the Dog is running around in the garden.

Digger: Birds can fly.
If I wave my paws,
maybe I can fly, too!

Chirpy the Bird flies into the garden.

Chirpy: Digger,
what are you doing?
Dogs can't fly!

Future Vocabulary

- Have children point to and read the chapter *title* on page 4. Then have them point to and read the *title* of the play (at the top of the script) on page 5. Ask *What do titles usually tell us?* (what the text is about)

- Discuss other alternate meanings for *titles*. Say *People who own land or cars have titles for their property. These titles tell who is the owner.*

Now revisit pages 6–7

During Reading

Book Talk
- Direct children's attention to the illustration on page 6. Ask *What are the children holding?* (their scripts) Read the names of the characters in the play as they are written on the actors' scripts. Point out to children that when they read a book, they should also read the words in the illustrations.

- **Phonics Skill** Read the first sentence on page 6. Say *Let's think of a word in the same family as* play. *Let's change the /p/ to /d/. What new word do we get?* (day)

Turn to page 8 — Book Talk

A Team of Helpers

Everyone in Maya's class helps put on the play.

Some children will be the actors. They will be the people and animals in the play.

6

Revisiting the Text

Some children will look after the lights. They will shine the lights on the stage.

Future Vocabulary

- Say *The picture on page 6 shows the* cast *for the play. There are four people in the* cast *of "The Dog Who Wanted to Fly."* Cast *is another way to refer to the actors in a play or movie.*

- Display the Meaning Map Interactive Modeling Card you started earlier in the lesson. Have children use *cast* in a sentence about actors in a play. Write one of the sentences in the Meaning Map. Have children help you complete the chart.

Now revisit pages 8–9

During Reading

Book Talk

- Read page 8 aloud. With children, compare and contrast these jobs with what actors do. Discuss how it takes many people to help put on a play, not just the actors.

- Read the first sentence on page 9. Explain that a set is how people make the stage look like the place in the play. Ask *How might a set of our classroom be different from the actual classroom?* (Instead of real books, the bookshelves would have books painted on them.)

- Ask *What does it mean to set the table?* (put out plates and silverware to prepare to eat)

Turn to page 10 – Book Talk

Some children will make sounds in the play. They will make lots of special noises.

Some children will make the **costumes**. Moms and dads will help them.

8

Revisiting the Text

Some children will build the **set**.
Moms and dads will help them, too.

The teacher will help everyone!

Future Vocabulary

- Have children locate the word *set* on page 9 and provide a definition. Refer to the glossary on page 24 and compare children's definition with the text definition.

- Introduce the word *scenery* and write it on the board. Explain that *scenery* can refer to the set for a play. *Scenery* can also mean natural surroundings. Give an example by saying the sentence *We enjoyed the scenery as we drove through the park.* Have children use *scenery* in a sentence about a place they have visited. Explain that *scenery* is usually used to describe places that are pleasing to look at.

Now revisit pages 10–11

During Reading

Book Talk

- Direct children's attention to the script illustrated on page 10. Review the parts of a script: the characters' names in boldfaced type, the lines actors speak onstage, and the stage directions in italics.

- Ask *What does it mean when someone writes in script?* (cursive writing; the letters connect to each other) Model the difference between writing in script and printing on the board. Ask children which way they prefer to write. Discuss why it is faster to write in script. (You don't need to stop at the end of each letter.)

Turn to page 12 — Book Talk

Chapter 4

Learning Lines

The words in a play script are called **lines**. Actors must remember their lines when they are in a play.

Mr. and Mrs. Johnson walk into the garden.
Chirpy the Bird is flying around.
Digger the Dog is trying to copy Chirpy.

Mrs. Johnson:
What is Digger doing?

Mr. Johnson:
I think he is trying to fly.
He is copying that bird.

Mrs. Johnson:
Silly Digger.
He is a dog, not a bird!

10

Revisiting the Text

Maya is going to be Mrs. Johnson in the play. She learns her lines.
The other actors learn their lines, too.

Future Vocabulary

- **Comprehension Strategy**
  Say *Look at page 11. The cast is rehearsing onstage. Which parts are they playing?* Have children go back to page 6 to reread the names of the characters.

Now revisit pages 12–13

During Reading

Book Talk

- Say *Page 12 shows the set for the play.* Point out the lighted area in the illustration on page 12. Ask *Why do you think this part is lighter than the rest?* (It shows where a light is shining.)

- **Phonics Skill** Read aloud the second sentence on page 13. Say *Let's add a sound to the word* up *to make a new word in the same family.* Write *up* on the board. Say *Let's add /k/ to the beginning. What new word do we get when we add /k/ to the beginning of* up? (*cup*) Discuss how both *k* and *c* can make /k/. Write the letter *c* before *up* on the board to spell *cup*.

- Ask *Do you think the audience will like the play? You could add that question or another one to your Activity Sheet.*

Turn to page 14 – Book Talk

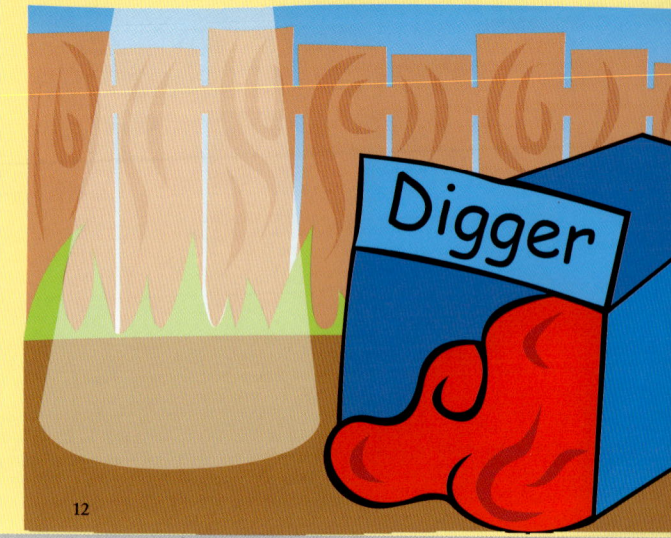

Revisiting the Text

Maya and her friends make a poster about the play.
The teacher puts up the poster.

COME TO OUR PLAY!

Friday night at 7 o'clock

Grade Two classroom

All welcome

Future Vocabulary
- Have children point to and read the chapter title on page 12. Have children name the titles of some of their favorite books and songs.

Now revisit pages 14–15

During Reading

Book Talk
- Have children point to the picture of the *set* on page 15. Discuss more alternate meanings for the word *set*. Ask *What is a tea set?* (the cups and saucers for serving tea) *A set can mean a group of things, like a tea set or a set of blocks.* Have children use the word *set* in a sentence.

Turn to page 16 – Book Talk

The Big Night

On the night of the play,
the actors put on their costumes.
They put on **makeup,** too.

Revisiting the Text

The **audience** sits in front of the stage. They wait for the play to begin.

Future Vocabulary

- Ask children to describe the scenery they see on page 15. (fence with grass and a doghouse for Digger)

Now revisit pages 16–17

During Reading

Book Talk

- Have children point to the actors on page 16. Ask *Are the boys on page 17 actors?* (no) *How do the actors look different from the others?* (They are wearing costumes.)

- Explain that putting on a play requires more people than actors. Tell children that these two boys are in charge of the music for the play.

Turn to page 18 – Book Talk

Revisiting the Text

Paula and Asha turn on the lights. Kelvin and Raj play some music. The play begins.

Future Vocabulary

- Say *Look at the boys who are playing music. Are these boys in the cast?* (no) *What title could they have?* (Sound Technician or Designer, Musician)

- Discuss alternate meanings for the word *cast*. Ask *What does it mean to cast when you are fishing?* (to throw a fishing line into the water)

Now revisit pages 18–19

During Reading

Book Talk
- Have children locate the word *actors* on page 19. Ask *How many actors are there in this play?* (four) *Why are there four actors?* (There are four parts in the *script*.)

- **Comprehension Strategy** Say *Look at the actors' costumes. Can you tell from the costumes which role each person is playing?* Remind children that they can go back and reread page 6 to find the answer.

Turn to page 20 – Book Talk

Chapter 7

Show Time!

Tony is Digger the Dog.
He runs around on the stage.
The audience laughs when he tries to fly.

Revisiting the Text

The other actors take their turns on the stage, too.
Everyone remembers their lines.

Future Vocabulary
- Direct children's attention to the scenery in the picture on page 19. The characters in this play are a dog, a bird, and a husband and wife.

- Ask *What kind of scenery would you expect to find in a play about a sailor?* (a boat, the ocean) *What kind of scenery would you expect to see in a play about going to the moon?* (a spaceship, outer space, the moon)

Now revisit pages 20–21

19

During Reading

Book Talk

- Ask *What happens when the play is over?* (The actors bow; the audience claps; all the children who worked on the play are onstage.) Together compare and contrast a play and a movie. (Both have actors and scripts; you watch live actors in a play.)

Turn to page 22 – Book Talk

The audience claps and cheers when the play is over.
The actors **bow** to the audience.
They are the stars of the show!

Revisiting the Text

The teacher takes some photos of the children. Moms and dads take some photos, too.

Future Vocabulary
- **Comprehension Strategy** Say *The cast is taking a bow. All the other people who helped put on the play are also taking a bow. Sometimes when the cast takes a bow, you can see scenery from the play. Can you see any scenery on these pages?* (no)

Now revisit pages 22–23

During Reading

Book Talk
- Leave this page spread for children to discover on their own when they read the book individually.

Turn to page 24 – Book Talk

After the play, there is a party. Everyone who helped with the play goes to the party.

Revisiting the Text

The class thanks the teacher for helping them with the play. They thank the moms and dads for helping them, too.

Putting on a play was lots of fun!

Future Vocabulary

- Say *Have you ever heard about something that is cast in stone? What does that mean?* (It is definite or certain.) *What things can you think of that are cast in stone?*

- Have children find a synonym for *cast* in the index. (actors) Have children find a synonym for *scenery* in the glossary. (set)

Go to page T5 – Revisiting the Text

During Reading

Book Talk
* Note: Point out this text feature page as a reference point for children's usage while reading independently.

Individual Reading
Have each child read the entire book at his or her own pace while remaining in the group.

Go to page T5 – Revisiting the Text

Glossary

actors	people who act out a story in a play
audience	the people who watch a play
backstage	a place behind the stage where actors and those working in a play go
bow	to bend from the waist, as a way of saying thank you
costumes	special clothes made for a play
lines	the words actors say in a play
makeup	special paints put on an actor's face
script	the words or story in a play
set	the part of a stage that is built to look like a place in a play
stage	a place (usually inside a building) where a play is held

Index

actors 2, 6, 10, 11, 14, 19, 20
audience 15, 18, 20
backstage 16
costumes 8, 12, 14
lights 7, 12, 17
lines 10–11, 19
makeup 14

parties 22–23
play poster 13
play script 4, 10
set 9, 12
sounds 8, 12, 17
stage 2, 7, 15, 18, 19
writing plays 4

24

During independent work time, children can read the online book at:
www.rigbyflyingcolors.com

24

Revisiting the Text

Future Vocabulary
- Use the notes on the right-hand pages to develop oral vocabulary that goes beyond the text. These vocabulary words first appear in future texts. These words are: *titles*, *scenery*, and *cast*.

Turn back to page 1

Reading Vocabulary Review
Activity Sheet: Word Sorter

- Have children complete the Word Sorter for *set*. In the second row of boxes, have children write *naming word* (noun) and *action or describing word* (verb or adjective).
- Tell children to think of words or phrases that describe *set* and write them under the appropriate category.

Comprehension Strategy Review
Use Interactive Modeling Card: Text Connections Web

- Read aloud the list of connection types at the top of the Text Connections Web. Model making a connection with the book's content and a personal experience of your own.
- Together fill in the Text Connections Web for *Stars of the Show*.

Phonics Review
- Write *all* on the board. Have children add phonemes to the beginning of *all* to make new words in the same family. *(call, tall, mall)*
- Discuss how changing the first letter of a word changes the meaning but keeps it in the same family. Use examples from the text, such as *night* to *light*.

Fluency Review
- Partner children and have them take turns reading pages 2–9. Remind them how to read smoothly by pausing at the appropriate places.
- Talk about why it is important to read smoothly.

Reading-Writing Connection
Activity Sheet: Questions and Answers Chart

To assist children with linking reading and writing:
- Have children complete the Questions and Answers Chart. Remind them to reread parts of the text to find the answers.
- Have children use information from their chart and from rereading the text to write a journal entry as if they were in the audience for the play performed in *Stars of the Show*.

4 Assessment

Assessing Future Vocabulary

Work with each child individually. Ask questions that elicit each child's understanding of the Future Vocabulary words. Note each child's responses:

- What are the titles of two books you can read yourself?
- What scenery would you expect to see on a drive through a forest?
- Which of these does *not* have a cast: a movie, a play, or a playground?

Assessing Comprehension Strategy

Work with each child individually. Ask questions and encourage them to go back and reread the text if they are unsure of the answer. Note each child's understanding of rereading text:

- What was the name of the dog in the play?
- How did the moms and dads help put on the play?
- Did anyone forget his or her lines during the play?
- Was each child able to go back to the text to find the answers to these questions?

Assessing Phonics

Work with each child individually. Have each child make new words by orally changing phonemes at the beginnings of words. Note each child's responses for understanding changing phonemes to create word families:

- Use these word groups: *-ig* (big — dig), *-ight* (light — night), *-ake* (take — cake).
- Was each child able to add phonemes to the beginnings of words to make new words?
- Did each child understand that phonemes can be added to the beginnings of words to make new words?

Assessing Fluency

Have each child read pages 2–5 to you. Note each child's understanding of reading smoothly:

- Was each child able to decode and accurately read the reading vocabulary words?
- Did each child wait until the end of the sentence before pausing to take a breath?

Interactive Modeling Cards

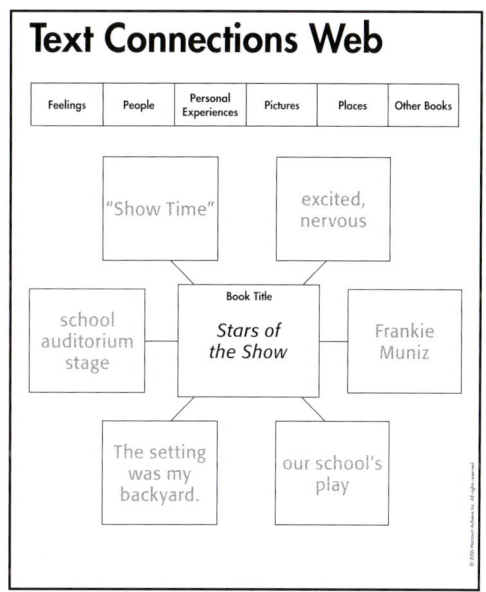

Directions: With children, fill in the Meaning Map using the word *cast*.

Directions: With children, fill in the Text Connections Web for *Stars of the Show*.

Discussion Questions
- What was the play about? (Literal)
- Why do people put on plays? (Critical Thinking)
- Why did some people take photographs at the end of the play? (Inferential)

T7

Activity Sheets

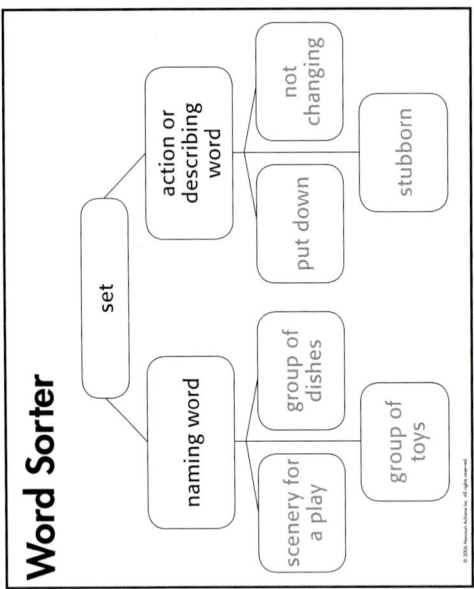

Directions: Have children fill in the Word Sorter for *set*, sorting phrases using the word *set* into naming words (nouns) and action or describing words (verbs or adjectives).

Directions: Have children fill in the Questions and Answers Chart for *Stars of the Show* and then use it to write a journal entry that an audience member might have written.

Optional: On a separate sheet of paper, have children write the title of a play they would like to write, a short description of what happens in their play, and a list of characters.

T8